Update Virginia

travel guide 2023

*Discover the Hidden Gems and Cultural Riches
of the Old Dominion State in this Authoritative
and Engaging Travel Companion*

Mary Homan

Copyright © 2023 Mary Homan

Table of contents

Introduction

We embarked on an absorbing tour through the Old Dominion in "Update Virginia Travel Guide 2023," a region rich in cultural diversity and steeped in history. Because of its illustrious past, stunning landscapes, and flourishing towns, Virginia offers a variety of exceptional experiences to both seasoned tourists and daring adventurers.

Chapter one

History of Virginia

Virginia's four-century history is a rich and intricate tapestry of events, people, and civilizations. From the earliest Native American tribes to the colonial era, the American Revolution, the Civil War, and beyond, Virginia has played an important role in shaping the course of American history.

The arrival of English colonists at Jamestown in 1607 was a watershed moment in Virginia history. The Virginia Company of London established the colony as a business venture to locate gold and silver to bring back to England. Surviving in the harsh Virginia wilderness, however, was tough, and the settlers relied on the adjacent Powhatan tribe for food and supplies.

Despite these challenges, the Jamestown community thrived, and by the mid-seventeenth century, Virginia had developed into a thriving tobacco region. As a result of the economic boom caused by Europe's desire for tobacco, large plantations maintained by enslaved Africans arose, establishing a system that would impact the region's social and economic structures for years to come.

Virginia was also crucial to the American Revolution. Many of the country's founding fathers were from Virginia, including George Washington, Thomas Jefferson, and James Madison, all of whom were instrumental in constructing the country's early administrative systems. A significant number of the Civil War's pivotal battles, such as Bull Run,

Fredericksburg, and Gettysburg, were fought on Virginian soil. The state also played an important role in the battle.

Throughout the twentieth century, Virginia has had a profound impact on American history. With significant events such as school desegregation in Prince Edward County in 1951 and lunch counter sit-ins in Richmond in 1960, the state served as a focal point for the Civil Rights movement. The Langley Research Center was an important hub for research and development, and Virginia also contributed significantly to the country's space program.

Geography and climate of Virginia

Geography

Virginia is a large state, covering approximately 42,775 square miles. It is located in the Appalachian Mountains, which run from Maine to Georgia. The majority of the eastern section of the state is a coastal plain with numerous tidal rivers and estuaries. Mount Rogers, the state's highest peak at 5,729 feet, is located in the state's western portion. The Shenandoah Valley is a rich agricultural region with numerous small towns and localities located between the Allegheny Mountains to the west and the Blue Ridge Mountains to the east.

Climate

The climate in Virginia varies greatly depending on where you are in the state. Virginia's eastern area has a humid subtropical climate, whilst its western region has a humid continental climate. Summers in the state's eastern area are hot and muggy, with highs and lows in the 80s and 90s Fahrenheit. Throughout the winter, temperatures frequently hover around 40 degrees Fahrenheit. The western section of the state has colder winters with regular lows below freezing, as well as milder summers with highs in the 70s and 80s Fahrenheit.

The coastal portions of Virginia are vulnerable to hurricanes, and the state has lately experienced several major hurricanes, including Hurricane Isabel in 2003 and Hurricane Irene in 2011. Tornadoes are another hazard in Virginia, where an average of 18 tornadoes occur each year.

In addition to hurricanes and tornadoes, Virginia is prone to earthquakes. Earthquakes have occurred in Virginia, albeit not as frequently as in other parts of the country. The most notable was the 2011 earthquake near Mineral, Virginia. The earthquake, which was felt as far away as New York City, caused significant damage to buildings and infrastructure in the state's central region.

Population and demographics of Virginia

Virginia's population has gradually increased during the previous few decades. According to the United States Census Bureau, Virginia's population increased by 7.9% between 2010 and 2020. In 2021, the state's population is expected to be 8,631,393. The majority of Virginia's population is centered in the eastern half of the state, which includes the Washington, D.C. metro region, Hampton Roads, and Richmond. Arlington is located in Northern Virginia.

Because of their proximity to Washington, D.C., and Fairfax counties have seen the most population growth over time.

Demographics:

In recent years, Virginia's population has seen significant change. According to the 2020 Census, Virginia's population is 51.2% female and 48.8% male. White non-Hispanics make up 62.5% of the state's population, making them the largest racial/ethnic group. Hispanics/Latinos account for 10.1% of the population, while African Americans account for 18.9%. Asians make up 7.4% of the population. The state's population is diverse, with a substantial proportion of citizens born outside of the country.

Age Distribution:

Virginia's population is getting older, with a median age of 38.7 years. According to the 2020 Census, there are 13.6% of those over the age of 65 and 22.9% of those under the age of 18. The working-age population in Virginia is 63.5%, meaning those between the ages of 18 and 64. As the need for elder services develops, the state's economy, healthcare system, and social services face challenges.

Education and Employment:

Virginia has a highly educated workforce, with over 40% of residents holding a bachelor's degree or above. The state is home to many notable universities, including the University of Virginia, Virginia Tech, and George Mason University. The government employs the most people in the state, followed by trade, transportation, utilities, professional and commercial services, education and health services, and trade. The state's unemployment rate in March 2021 was 4.0%, which was lower than the national average of 6.0%.

Chapter two

Planning Your Trip

When to visit Virginia

When planning a trip to Virginia, one of the most important factors to consider is the weather. Virginia's weather is infamous for being erratic, with hot, steamy summers and freezing winters. The best times to visit Virginia are in the spring and October.

Because of the mild temperatures and low humidity, the spring season in Virginia (March to May) is great for seeing the state's natural beauty. Virginians residing close to Washington, D.C. can also attend the renowned Cherry Blossom Festival during this season.

Fall (September to November) is the finest time to experience Virginia's scenic grandeur since the weather begins to cool and the leaves begin to change color. During this season, there are also a variety of celebrations and events, such as the Virginia State Fair in Doswell and the Shenandoah Apple Blossom Festival in Winchester.

Peak Tourist Seasons:

When making travel arrangements to Virginia, keep peak tourist season in mind. From June to August, Virginia has its biggest travel season. At this time of year, the weather is hot and steamy, and travelers flock to Virginia's beaches and theme parks. This, however, may result in higher housing expenses and longer wait times at attractions.

If you want to avoid crowds during the summer, consider visiting on a weekday. Consider going during the shoulder season, which runs from early June to late August, when the weather is still pleasant but there are fewer tourists.

Events and Festivals:

Finally, when planning a trip to Virginia, keep in mind the numerous events and festivals that take place throughout the year. Virginia has numerous cultural and historical events, such as the Virginia Wine Festival in September and the Virginia International Tattoo in April.

The anniversary of the arrival of the first Africans in English North America in 1619 is one of the most significant dates in Virginia's history. The 400th anniversary of this historic event was marked in 2019 by a series of events dubbed "American Evolution." Although this anniversary has passed, Virginia's long history is still commemorated annually through a variety of cultural and historical activities.

Virginia has several airports that serve both domestic and international flights, including Ronald Reagan Washington National Airport, Washington Dulles International Airport, Richmond International Airport, Norfolk International Airport, and Newport News/Williamsburg International Airport. Because these airports are dispersed throughout the state, it is critical to select the one that is nearest to your location.

How to get to Virginia

By Car: Travelers might also choose to drive to Virginia. Major highways including I-95, I-81, I-64, and the Virginia Beach-Norfolk Expressway make it easy to get to the state. The most popular entrance point for visitors from the north is I-95, which runs from Maine to Florida and through Virginia. Drivers arriving from the south can enter Virginia via I-85 or I-77.

By Train: Amtrak's train network serves several Virginia cities, including Alexandria, Richmond, Newport News, and Norfolk. The Amtrak Carolinian route connects Virginia with cities in North Carolina and New York, whereas the Amtrak Northeast Regional route travels from Boston to Virginia with several stops in between.

By bus: Several bus companies, including Greyhound, Megabus, and Trailways, offer service to Virginia. These companies operate routes that connect major cities in the Northeast, Midwest, and Virginia.

You may get around Virginia using a variety of transportation choices once you arrive. The Virginia Department of Transportation operates a network of roadways, bridges, and tunnels that connect towns and cities throughout the state. Public transportation options vary by location, however, many cities have bus and light rail service. In the majority of cities, you can also use taxis and ride-sharing services.

Passport and visa requirements

To begin, it is critical to understand that the United States has stringent entry requirements for foreign nationals, including the necessity for them to have a valid passport as well as a visa or other form of permitted travel. All foreign nationals entering the United States, regardless of the reason for their visit, are required to have a passport. A passport serves as identification as well as proof of citizenship and entry eligibility into a country.

Foreign nationals may also need a visa to enter the United States, depending on their country of origin and the purpose of their visit. The United States government gives visas to foreign nationals to allow them to visit the country for a limited time and a defined purpose. In some circumstances, certain eligible people may be permitted to visit the United States without a visa thanks to a visa waiver program.

Foreign nationals entering Virginia should ensure that their passport is valid for the duration of their stay. Foreign nationals may also be required to obtain a visa, depending on their place of origin and the purpose of their trip. The type of visa you require will depend on whether you are going for business, leisure, or education. It is critical to contact the US Embassy or Consulate in the country of origin for detailed information on visa requirements for entry into the United States.

The United States has strict entry processes, and foreign nationals must ensure that they follow all requirements to enter the country. Failure to meet the admission standards may result in denial of entry, deportation, or legal consequences. Foreign nationals should carefully evaluate the entrance requirements before traveling to Virginia or any other state in the United States.

Budgeting for your trip

The first step in developing a budget for a vacation to Virginia is determining how long and how many people will be traveling. This will aid in the establishment of the budget's core framework. For

For example, if the trip is a weeklong family vacation for four people, the budget must cover their food, accommodation, transportation, and entertainment for the full week.

The next step is to research and estimate the costs associated with each component of the trip. This includes flight or petrol expenses, housing expenses like hotels or vacation rentals, transportation expenses like taxis or public transit, food and beverage prices, and any planned entertainment or activities.

Making a more exact and complete budget plan can be aided by researching various options and weighing prices.

Budget for unexpected costs that may arise during the trip, such as emergency medical fees, lost or stolen possessions, or changes to the intended travel schedule. Setting aside money from the budget for such unanticipated charges may lessen stress in the event of an emergency.

Taking advantage of discounts and special offers is an important consideration when establishing a budget for a vacation to Virginia. This can include pre-purchasing attraction tickets, using credit cards with travel advantages, or finding accommodations with discounted rates. Taking advantage of such discounts can help stretch the budget even further and reduce the overall cost of the holiday.

Recommended travel insurance

When choosing a travel insurance plan, it's critical to consider the coverage options and constraints of each policy. Tourists may require medical attention while in Virginia due to the high cost of medical care. Pre-existing medical issues, as well as medical crises, should be covered by a comprehensive travel insurance plan, as should the cost of evacuation and repatriation.

Another important consideration is trip cancellation or interruption insurance. Flights may be delayed or canceled owing to unanticipated weather conditions due to Virginia's fickle weather. Unexpected incidents such as illness or accident may also prohibit a traveler from starting a trip. Non-refundable expenditures such as airline tickets, hotel reservations, and vacation packages may be covered by a travel insurance policy that includes trip cancellation or interruption coverage.

Lost or stolen luggage is another potential concern that travel insurance may cover. Comprehensive travel insurance coverage should cover the cost of lost or stolen luggage, including personal things such as cameras, laptops, and other electronic devices.

When selecting travel insurance, it is critical to consider the insurance company's reputation and financial stability. A reliable insurance company should have a track record of handling customer claims quickly and efficiently. In addition, the insurance company should have a solid financial base and the resources to cover claims in the event of a big disaster.

Visitors to Virginia are encouraged to obtain one of the many comprehensive travel insurance policies offered by insurance providers. One of the most popular options is the Allianz Global Assistance Travel Insurance Plan, which covers medical emergencies, trip cancellation or interruption, and lost or stolen luggage. The package also includes access to a network of medical providers, customer service, and assistance 24 hours a day, seven days a week.

Another option is the Travel Guard Essential Plan, which covers medical emergencies, trip cancellation or interruption, and lost or stolen luggage. In addition, the plan includes concierge services, identity theft resolution choices, and emergency travel assistance.

Chapter three

Accommodations

Overview of accommodation options in Virginia Hotels are the most popular type of lodging in Virginia, and prices range from low-cost motels to sumptuous five-star places. Room service, a gym, a business center, and a restaurant are usually available in these establishments. They are almost everywhere in the state and offer guests a practical and comfortable place to stay. Some of Virginia's most well-known hotel brands are Marriott, Hilton, and Hyatt.

Motels are another popular option for visitors searching for low-cost lodging. These establishments are ideal for people on a short budget because they generally offer smaller rooms and fewer amenities than hotels. Free parking is a typical amenity provided by motels, which can be a significant benefit for those who drive. Virginia has some motels, particularly along its busy highways and interstates.

Resorts are another popular hotel option in Virginia, particularly around the shore. Swimming pools, tennis courts, golf courses, and spas are common features of these establishments. They could be an excellent choice for families or couples looking for a peaceful retreat or a passionate getaway. Some of Virginia's most well-known resorts are The Homestead, Kingsmill Resort, and Salamander Resort & Spa.

Vacation rentals are becoming increasingly popular among travelers, particularly those looking for a more homelike experience. These accommodations, which range from apartments and condos to homes and villas, can be rented for short-term trips. Vacation rentals give guests a lot of freedom by allowing them to prepare their meals, do their laundry, and live like locals. Airbnb, VRBO, and HomeAway are platforms for renting out vacation properties.

Top hotels and resorts

The Williamsburg Inn, located in the heart of Colonial Williamsburg, is at the top of our list. This elegant hotel has attracted many prominent visitors, including Queen Elizabeth II and Prince Philip, since its creation in 1937. The Williamsburg Inn has luxury features such as an indoor pool.

a championship golf course, a full-service spa, and an award-winning restaurant. Guests can also take advantage of free transportation to nearby attractions such as the historic Jamestown Settlement.

The 340-acre Salamander Resort and Spa in Middleburg, Virginia, is up next. This lovely resort offers a tranquil haven with a focus on relaxation and well-being. The Salamander Resort & Spa features a championship golf course, a superb spa, and an equestrian complex. Visitors can also take lessons and ride on the trails. Aside from wine tastings at surrounding vineyards, the resort also offers farm-to-table cuisine.

Our next stop is the Ritz-Carlton, Tysons Corner, which is near Washington, D.C. This luxurious hotel features luxury extras such as a 24-hour fitness center, a full-service spa, and an indoor pool. The Ritz-Carlton, Tysons Corner is well-known for its excellent dining options, which include a variety of cafes serving modern

American cuisine and flavors from across the world.

Another prominent hotel in Virginia is the Jefferson Hotel, which is located in the heart of Richmond. This old hotel, built in 1895, has been restored to its former glory. The Jefferson Hotel's luxurious amenities include a full-service spa, an indoor pool, and a fitness center. Guests can also dine at the hotel's award-winning restaurant Lemaire, which serves a modern spin on Southern cuisine.

Bed and breakfasts

Bed & breakfasts became popular in the early twentieth century as vacationers sought a more intimate and personalized vacation experience. B&Bs have their origins in Virginia's colonial history when travelers would seek out the goodwill of residents in exchange for a bed for the night and a hearty breakfast the next day.

Since this tradition has persisted, Virginia now has hundreds of B&Bs, each with its distinct charm and personality.

Amenities Offered by Virginia Bed and Breakfasts

Virginia B&Bs offer comfortable housing, tasty meals, and attentive service to their guests. Many bed and breakfasts in Virginia are set in renovated farmhouses or historic plantation homes. These structures usually include great interior design, such as antique furniture and artwork, which adds to the attractiveness and mood of the residence.

In addition to excellent lodging, Virginia B&Bs usually feature several extras such as free Wi-Fi, cable TV, and in-room fireplaces. In addition, some B&Bs provide visitors with access to outdoor activities such as golfing, fishing, and hiking trails.

Cultural Significance of Virginia Bed and Breakfasts

B&Bs in Virginia are culturally significant because they allow visitors to experience the state's particular history and culture. Many Virginia bed and breakfasts are located in or near historic or culturally significant sites, allowing tourists to learn about the state's rich legacy and history. Tourists staying at Charlottesville's Inn at Monticello, for example, have the opportunity to see Thomas Jefferson's home, one of the country's founding fathers.

Hostels

A hostel is a type of low-cost lodging that provides guests with public facilities, self-catering kitchens, and shared dormitory-style rooms. In response to the need for inexpensive housing among young travelers, Germany saw the construction of the first hostels early in the twentieth century. Since then, hostels have grown throughout Europe and the rest of the world, offering budget travelers a unique opportunity to engage with people from many nationalities and cultures.

Many hostels now provide private rooms with en-suite bathrooms, as well as other amenities such as free Wi-Fi, laundry facilities, and even on-site bars and restaurants. Hostels have changed dramatically throughout the years. Hostels are becoming increasingly diverse and serve a wide range of passengers, including families, senior citizens, and backpackers.

Hostels can be found across Virginia, from populated towns such as Richmond and Norfolk to isolated areas such as the Shenandoah Valley. Many of these hostels offer moderate costs and unique sleeping alternatives, such as ancient mansions transformed into hostels or jails.

One such example is the Hostelling International Richmond hostel, which is housed in a former mansion in the famed Fan District. This hostel offers both private and communal rooms, as well as a common lounge and kitchen. Another example is the HI Richmond Downtown hostel, which is centrally located and features both private and communal rooms, as well as a rooftop patio and a bar.

Hostels can give unique cultural experiences by sponsoring a variety of activities such as culinary courses, language exchanges, and cultural tours. For example, the International Hostel in Norfolk hosts activities such as a weekly International Night where guests may learn about different cultures through music and food.

Hostels have many benefits, but they also have some drawbacks. While some tourists may feel uncomfortable sharing a room with others in a dormitory-style arrangement, others may prefer the isolation and luxury of a hotel. However, hostels may not be suitable for persons with mobility issues or those seeking a more upscale experience.

Campgrounds

Types of Campgrounds:

In Virginia, there are various campgrounds, each with unique features and services. Some of the more popular camping types in Virginia are: State Park Campgrounds - Virginia has 38 state parks, many of which contain campgrounds. State park campgrounds are often well-maintained and include a variety of amenities such as showers, power, and water hookups, and even Wi-Fi.

Campgrounds in National Parks: Shenandoah National Park, one of many national parks in Virginia, offers several campgrounds. State park campgrounds are often more modern, with fewer amenities but more magnificent landscapes; national park campgrounds are typically more basic, with fewer amenities but more breathtaking scenery.

Private Campgrounds - Virginia has a variety of private campgrounds, most of which are owned by individuals or businesses. These campgrounds usually include more amenities, such as swimming pools, playgrounds, and organized activities, than state or national park campgrounds.

Features of Campgrounds:

Every campground in Virginia has its unique set of amenities and activities. Some of the most popular amenities in Virginia campgrounds include:

Many Virginia campgrounds offer amazing views of the surrounding terrain, which includes mountains, lakes, and rivers. These panoramas provide visitors with the opportunity to relax and enjoy the beauty and calm of nature.

Outdoor Activities - Hiking, fishing, boating, and swimming are just a few of the outdoor activities accessible in Virginia campsites. Visitors can appreciate Virginia's natural beauty while also gaining some fitness by participating in these activities.

Historical Sites - Because Virginia is rich in history, there are numerous campgrounds nearby. These sites allow visitors to learn about the state's history and the role it played in the formation of the United States.

Chapter four

Dining and Nightlife

Virginia's culinary scene

One of Virginia's most well-known meals is country ham, a salt-cured pig dish that has been a staple of southern cuisine for centuries. The ham is usually served thinly sliced in numerous restaurants throughout the state. Another popular snack is Virginia-style peanuts, which are roasted with their skins on and have a particularly crunchy texture.

Given Virginia's 3,000 miles of Atlantic Ocean and Chesapeake Bay coastline, seafood plays an important role in the state's gastronomic environment. Chesapeake Bay blue crabs are delicious steamed or in recipes like crab cakes and crab soup. Virginia produces over 500 million oysters each year and is well-known for its love of oyster recipes.

They go well with craft beer or wine and can be served raw, steamed, fried, or grilled.

In addition to its seafood, Virginia is well-known for its barbeque, with each region having its particular style. While the western half of the state is famous for its tomato-based sauce, the eastern half is famed for its vinegar-based sauce. Briskets, ribs, and pulled pork are all common items on barbecue menus.

Farm-to-table restaurants have become more common in Virginia's culinary scene, and many chefs now employ ingredients grown locally.

This trend has aided small-scale farmers throughout the state while also promoting sustainable agriculture. Restaurants like The Roosevelt in Richmond and The Shack in Staunton have become popular hangouts for foodies looking for a taste of Virginia's farm-fresh cuisine.

Because of its number of craft breweries and over 300 wineries, Virginia is a popular destination for wine and beer enthusiasts. The state's wine sector has recently garnered notoriety, with certain vineyards winning awards at international competitions. Breweries such as The Veil Brewing Co. in Richmond and Hardywood Park Craft Brewery in Charlottesville are attracting national notice, and Virginia's craft beer scene is growing.

Best restaurants and cafes

One of Virginia's best restaurants is The Inn at Little Washington, located in the charming town of Washington. This Michelin-starred restaurant is well-known for its excellent cuisine, luxurious atmosphere, and impeccable service. The menu features a wide range of dishes, including vegetarian, meat, and seafood options, all prepared with the finest regional ingredients. Among the highlight dishes are the foie gras terrine, seared scallops, and roasted duck breast.

L'Auberge Provencale, a beautiful country pub that you must visit while in Virginia, is a must-see. Traditional French dishes are made with a modern touch using fresh, regional ingredients in this French-themed restaurant. Escargots, bouillabaisse, and rack of lamb are just a few of the delectable delicacies available.

Virginia has a plethora of cafes that provide wonderful food and have a pleasant environment for those seeking a more informal dining experience. The Little Grill Collective, a Harrisonburg café, is one of the best in Virginia. This locally-owned cafe offers vegetarian and vegan options in addition to standard American fare. The menu items, which include vegan chili, falafel wraps, and huevos rancheros, are all made with high-quality ingredients and served in generous portions.

Another well-known cafe in Virginia is the Tandem Friends School Cafe in Charlottesville. This student-run cafe serves organic and locally sourced foods such as soups, sandwiches, and salads.

Salads are also available. The cafe also has a seasonal menu, so there is always something new and interesting to try.

Even though these are some of the best restaurants in Virginia, it's important to note that the state is home to a plethora of other excellent establishments. From farm-to-table eateries in the Shenandoah Valley to seafood shacks on the Eastern Shore, Virginia has something for everyone's taste and budget.

Bars and nightlife options

Virginia's pubs and nightlife options range from busy metropolises like Richmond and Virginia Beach to beautiful rural villages like Charlottesville and Williamsburg. Virginia offers them all, whether you want a cool rooftop bar with panoramic views, a cozy pub with live music, or a frenzied dance club.

Richmond, Virginia's state capital, is one of the most popular nightlife destinations. The city has a thriving pub scene, with selections to suit any taste or mood. One of Richmond's top bars is The Jasper, a tiny cocktail bar that specializes in classic drinks made with fresh, regional ingredients. Another popular option is the Hof Garden, a large beer garden with live music and a rotating selection of specialty brews.

Numerous bars and clubs line the boardwalk on Virginia Beach's coastal strip, which is a popular nighttime destination. One of the most popular venues is Peabody's Nightclub, which has multiple dance floors, live music, and themed parties. For a more casual experience, go to Esoteric, a craft beer pub with a vast selection of unique and hard-to-find brews.

If you want a more affluent experience, go to Charlottesville, which is home to the University of Virginia and a thriving arts and entertainment scene. There are several upmarket cocktail bars in the neighborhood, including the C&O Restaurant and Bar, which is housed in a former train station and provides a sophisticated menu of beverages and small meals. Another option is The Alley Light, a tiny speakeasy-style pub with expertly prepared cocktails and a rotating selection of wines.

Of course, every nocturnal situation has potential disadvantages. One of these worries is the dangers of binge drinking and the negative consequences it can have, such as impaired judgment, accidents, and health problems. Furthermore, some people may find the more dominating or uncomfortable aspects of nightlife, such as loud music and crowded areas, to be off-putting. It's vital to be aware of these potential dangers and to take the required precautions, such as limiting alcohol consumption and choosing situations that feel safe and welcome.

Chapter five

Things to Do

Top attractions in Virginia

One of Virginia's most well-known landmarks is the historic Jamestown Settlement, the first permanent English settlement in North America. Being able to travel back in time and Court House National Historical Park, where General Robert E. Lee surrendered to General Ulysses S. Grant, is another must-see for Civil War enthusiasts.

Museums:

Virginia also has a variety of museums dedicated to the state's history. The Virginia Museum of History and Culture in Richmond features exhibits on topics such as Virginia's role in the Civil War, its aboriginal peoples, and its contributions to the foundation of the country. In Richmond, the Museum of the Confederacy has exhibits about the war, its generals, and its troops, with a focus on the Confederate States of America.

The Virginia Aviation Museum, located near Richmond International Airport, explores the state's contributions to aviation history. Visitors can see a variety of aircraft, including early experimental models and modern jets, and learn more about aviation pioneers. For those interested in African American history, the Virginia Museum of Fine Arts in Richmond has a permanent collection of works by African

American artists as well as rotating exhibits on the subject.

Nature and outdoor activities

Hiking is one of Virginia's most popular outdoor activities. There are numerous hiking trails around the state, ranging from easy nature hikes to strenuous mountain climbs. The Appalachian Trail, which passes through Virginia and affords hikers with breathtaking views of the Blue Ridge Mountains, spans 2,200 miles from Georgia to Maine. Great Falls Park, which features spectacular waterfalls, and Shenandoah National Park, which has over 500 miles of hiking trails, are two more popular hiking sites.

Camping is another popular outdoor activity in Virginia. There are around 35 national forests and state parks with camping spots in the state. These campgrounds are located in some of the most scenic areas of the state, including the Shenandoah Valley and the Blue Ridge Mountains. Campers can enjoy activities such as swimming, hiking, and fishing while enjoying the peace of the outdoors.

Because Virginia has so many rivers, streams, and lakes, fishing is a favorite sport there. Many fish species can be found in the state, including trout, bass, and catfish. Some of Virginia's most popular fishing spots are the James River, the New River, and Lake Anna.

Boating is another popular outdoor activity in Virginia, because of the state's large coastline and several lakes and rivers. Boaters can enjoy leisure activities like sailing, kayaking, and water skiing while observing the beauty of the natural surroundings. Boaters routinely visit the Chesapeake Bay, one of the world's largest estuaries.

In addition to physical benefits, outdoor activities have been shown to improve mental health. Spending time outdoors has been found to improve mood, creativity, and stress levels. This is due to the relaxing effect of natural settings, which can reduce the release of stress hormones and increase feelings of well-being.

retail as well as entertainment

Chapter six

Festivals and Events

Overview of the annual events and festivals in Virginia

The Virginia Beach Neptune Festival, held in September, is one of Virginia's most popular celebrations. The festival, which coincides with the start of fall and the end of summer, features a parade, live music performances, arts and crafts exhibits, food vendors, and other activities. The festival includes the famed Neptune Cup Sand Soccer Tournament, which attracts soccer fans from all over the world.

Another notable event in Virginia is the Virginia Wine Festival, which takes place in October. Visitors to the event can sample and purchase wines from more than 20 Virginia wineries, as well as enjoy live entertainment, food vendors, and seminars on wine production and tasting. The festival celebrates Virginia's thriving wine industry, which has seen remarkable growth in recent years.

For history aficionados, the annual "Military Through the Ages" event at the Jamestown Settlement is a must-see. The March event features reenactors from several historical eras, including the American Civil War, the Renaissance, and the Middle Ages. The reenactors exhibit their military prowess and historical knowledge, providing tourists with a unique and educational experience.

Along with these events, Virginia hosts a variety of festivals throughout the year to celebrate its cultural diversity. For example, the annual International Festival, held in October, has performances and displays from over 50 different countries, including food, dance, and music. The Richmond Folk Festival, which also takes place in October, showcases musicians from many genres such as bluegrass, gospel, and Cajun.

Traveling with Kids

Family-friendly attractions in Virginia

The Virginia Aquarium & Marine Science Center in Virginia Beach is one of the top places in Virginia to take children. At this interactive museum with a variety of marine exhibitions, visitors may get up close and personal with aquatic wildlife such as sharks, sea turtles, and rays. The museum also offers a range of educational events and kid-friendly activities, making it an excellent spot to spend a family day.

Another popular tourist attraction in Richmond is the Science Museum of Virginia. A planetarium, an interactive displays section, and live science demonstrations are just a few of the exhibits and events available at this interactive science and technology museum. It's a great place for families with kids of all ages to learn about everything from physics and chemistry to biology and astronomy.

Shenandoah National Park is a must-see destination for families who want to explore the great outdoors. The park, located in Virginia's Blue Ridge Mountains, features miles of hiking trails, breathtaking views, and scenic roads. Visitors can enjoy camping, picnicking, and a range of recreational activities such as horseback riding, bird watching, and fishing.

For thrill-seekers, Busch Gardens in Williamsburg is an excellent choice. This amusement park includes live entertainment and animal exhibitions in addition to roller coasters and other thrilling rides. The park also has a variety of family-friendly attractions, such as child rides and a Sesame Street-themed play area.

Recommended activities for children

Children are society's backbone, and a thriving community cannot exist without protecting their health and well-being. Participating in a variety of activities can enhance their social skills, cognitive development, and physical and mental health. In Virginia, children can participate in many enjoyable and instructive activities.

Outdoor Activities:

Because of its natural beauty and pleasant climate, Virginia is an excellent destination for outdoor activities. Families will like the state's many parks, beaches, and hiking trails. Swimming, surfing, kayaking, and paddleboarding are among the water sports available at Virginia Beach, which is located on the Atlantic Ocean. Shenandoah National Park in the Blue Ridge Mountains has stunning views and over 500 miles of hiking trails. Families can also visit numerous campgrounds, fishing holes, and wildlife refuges.

Arts & Culture:

Because of Virginia's unique cultural past, children have numerous opportunities to participate in the arts. The enormous collection of world art at the Virginia Museum of Fine Arts in Richmond includes paintings, sculptures, and decorative arts. Children may learn about marine life and the environment through interactive displays at Virginia Beach's Virginia Aquarium and Marine Science Center. Additionally, the Virginia Symphony Orchestra and the Virginia Opera present family-friendly concerts throughout the year.

Sports and fitness:

Physical activity is beneficial to children's health and well-being, and Virginia offers numerous opportunities for children to participate in sports and fitness activities. Throughout the state, there are numerous parks and leisure centers that offer sports leagues, fitness programs, and summer camps. The Virginia High School League allows children of various ages to compete in sports such as football, basketball, soccer, and track and field. Every year, Virginia also hosts a variety of cycling, triathlon, and marathon competitions.

Educational Activities:

Virginia has several educational institutions where children can learn about science, history, and culture. Virginia has a diverse cultural background. The Virginia Museum of Science is located in Richmond, Virginia.

Richmond's interactive displays and programs teach children about science and technology. Visitors to the Jamestown Settlement and the Colonial Williamsburg Foundation, both of which offer historical reenactments and displays, can learn about Virginia's early history. The Natural Bridge Zoo and the Virginia Zoo in Norfolk are both great places for kids to learn about nature and conservation.

Chapter seven

Safety and Health

Tips for staying safe in Virginia

Be aware of your surroundings:
Being aware of your surroundings is one of the most important safety tips for Virginia

residents. This requires being aware of the people, places, and objects around you.

By being aware of potential risks in your environment, you can notice them and take action to avoid them.

Another important piece of advice for being safe in Virginia is to apply common sense. For example, never leave valuables unattended in your car, lock your windows and doors at home, and avoid venturing out at night alone in unusual places. By using common sense, you can reduce your chances of becoming a victim of crime.

Stay informed: Keeping informed is an important aspect of staying safe in Virginia. This requires learning about local risks and hazards, as well as current local news and happenings. By staying informed, you can take the necessary steps and avoid potentially hazardous circumstances.

Trusting your instincts is essential for being safe in Virginia. If something appears to be strange, trust your intuition and take measures. This could include fleeing a dangerous situation or seeking aid from a trustworthy authority source.

It is essential to adopt proper cyber hygiene: Proper cyber hygiene is equally important in today's digital world. This includes using safe passwords, avoiding public Wi-Fi, and exercising caution when revealing personal information online. By using these protections, you can protect yourself against identity theft and other online threats.

Last but not least, being prepared for catastrophes is vital. This comprises having a plan in place in case of natural disasters or other calamities, such as knowing the best evacuation routes and keeping an emergency kit fully packed. Being prepared can lower your chance of danger or injury in an emergency circumstance.

Information on healthcare facilities and services

There are numerous types of healthcare facilities in Virginia, including hospitals, clinics, and nursing homes. Virginia has 105 hospitals with various specialties such as trauma centers, children's hospitals, and cancer centers. In addition to hospitals, Virginia has a large number of urgent care centers and outpatient clinics that provide medical care for minor diseases and accidents. Nursing homes are long-term care facilities that provide specialized nursing care and rehabilitation services.

The University of Virginia Health System and the Virginia Commonwealth University Health System are two academically affiliated hospitals in Virginia. These hospitals specialize in areas such as pediatric care, organ transplantation, and cancer treatment and research.

Healthcare Services:

Virginia provides primary care, specialty care, preventative care, and mental health therapies. Primary care includes routine check-ups, physicals, and the management of chronic conditions such as diabetes and hypertension. Specialty care services are available for certain medical disorders such as cardiology and gastroenterology.

Preventative care refers to services that promote healthy behaviors and illness prevention. Cancer screenings, immunizations, and health information are among the services provided.

There are also mental health clinics in Virginia that provide therapy and counseling for diseases such as depression and anxiety.

Access to Healthcare:

Although Virginia offers healthcare facilities and services, some people and communities are concerned about healthcare access. Geographical location, linguistic barriers, and socioeconomic status all have an impact on access to healthcare. Medicaid and the Virginia Free Clinic Network are only two of the state of Virginia's initiatives and programs aimed at improving healthcare access.

Chapter height

Useful websites and apps

The Virginia 511 app is one of the most popular and useful apps in Virginia. This app keeps Virginia residents up to date on traffic, crashes, construction, and road closures. Users can also view traffic cameras and receive customized travel notifications. The Virginia 511 app can help commuters and tourists alike plan their travels more efficiently and avoid delays.

Another useful tool for folks who live in Virginia is MyVirginia. This app provides access to a range of state services, including DMV services, tax services, and public safety information. Users can also use it to track the status of their tax refunds and receive updates about them.Important deadlines.

The MyVirginia app makes it simple and convenient to access critical government services.

The Virginia Museum of History & Culture website is an excellent resource for anybody interested in learning more about Virginia's rich history and culture. The website has a wealth of historical information, including displays, relics, and instructional resources. It also conducts some online events and programs, making it a convenient and engaging way to learn about Virginia's past.

The Virginia Department of Health website is another useful resource for Virginia residents. This page contains up-to-date information on public health problems, including COVID-19. It also offers tools and resources to help you stay healthy, such as information on immunizations, nutrition, and mental health. Anyone interested in staying up to date on Virginia public health problems may visit the Virginia Department of Health website.

The Virginia Tech Department of Psychology website is a valuable resource for psychology researchers and students. The website contains information on faculty specializations, academic programs, and research opportunities. It also provides access to a wide range of resources, such as databases, publications, and research tools. Anyone interested in psychology should visit the Virginia Tech Department of Psychology website.

While these websites and apps have a lot to offer Virginia residents, it's important to recognize that they also have some disadvantages. For example, some users may find the Virginia 511 app complicated to use. Similarly, not all features that particular users require may be available on the MyVirginia app.

Furthermore, some users may believe that the Virginia Museum of History & Culture website is overly focused on traditional historical interpretations and would prefer to see more nuanced analyses of Virginia's past.

Emergency contacts

To begin with, it is critical to recognize that having an emergency contact is not required by Virginia law. Having an emergency contact, on the other hand, can be highly useful in catastrophic situations. Many hospitals and healthcare facilities in Virginia will ask people for the phone number or email address of a relative or friend who may be called in the event of an emergency.

When choosing an emergency contact, a variety of factors must be considered. Emergency contact should preferably be someone you know who is available in the event of an emergency.

Furthermore, this person should be able and willing to make critical decisions for you if you are unable to do so on your own.

Consider establishing an advance medical directive in addition to providing your contact information to a friend or family member. In this legal document, you can express your preferences for medical care and end-of-life care. In Virginia, an advance medical directive must be signed in the presence of two witnesses or a notary public.

It is also worth noting that Virginia law allows persons to choose an agent to make healthcare decisions on their behalf. This can be accomplished with a durable power of attorney for healthcare. You can name a trusted individual in this agreement to make essential medical decisions on your behalf if you become incapacitated.

It's important to remember that the Health Insurance Portability and Accountability Act (HIPAA) safeguards the privacy of medical information. This means that healthcare practitioners are not allowed to divulge their medical information to anyone unless you permit them. Your designated emergency contact or healthcare agent may have access to your medical records in the case of an emergency.

Language guide

One of the primary roles of language guides in Virginia is to assist non-native speakers in navigating the English language. This can include providing translation services, interpreting for non-native speakers at meetings or court proceedings, and assisting with paperwork or documents that require English fluency. Language learning tools also provide relevant cultural knowledge that can help non-native speakers comprehend the nuances of communication in Virginia.

Although language guides serve an important role in the community, they face a variety of challenges. One of the key challenges is a lack of funding and support for language programs. Because many language instructors are volunteers or work on a shoestring budget, providing the tools needed for effective communication may be difficult. Furthermore, there is a scarcity of professional language guides who can successfully communicate with non-native speakers and speak multiple languages fluently.

Despite these challenges, language guides in Virginia provide a variety of benefits to the community. One of the most significant benefits for non-native speakers is access to resources and services.

Language aids can expand everyone's access to these resources by supporting non-native speakers in navigating the complex systems of healthcare, education, and government services. Language aids can also help non-native speakers integrate into their surroundings, reducing social isolation and improving overall quality of life.

Furthermore, research in the fields of psychology and cognitive science has revealed the numerous cognitive and social benefits of being bilingual. Bilingual persons are better at paying attention, multitasking, and problem-solving. Virginians who are not native English speakers can reap these cognitive and social benefits by learning the language and becoming bilingual.

Currency and tipping information

Virginia, like the rest of the United States, uses the US dollar as its official currency. The US dollar is accepted by the majority of companies in Virginia, including restaurants, motels, and tourist attractions. The introduction of the US dollar

There are bills of $1, $5, $10, $20, $50, and $100 available. Coins with denominations of 1 cent, 5 cents, 10 cents, 25 cents, and 50 cents are also available. These coins are known as pennies, nickels, dimes, quarters, and half-dollars.

It's critical to remember that exchange rates in Virginia can fluctuate depending on where you are and how much you're converting. It's also worth noting that some shops may not accept travelers' checks or other foreign currencies, so having US dollars on hand is usually a good idea.

Tipping Practices in Virginia

Tipping is customary in the service industry, and Virginia is no exception. In general, tips are expected for services such as meals, haircuts, and spa visits. The amount of the tip varies depending on the industry and the quality of the service. In general, waiters, bartenders, and delivery drivers are often tipped between 15% and 20% of the overall cost of eating services.

For haircuts and other personal grooming services, the standard tip is between 15% and 20% of the total service charge. The standard gratuity for spa treatments is between 15% and 20% of the total cost of the service, with certain institutions suggesting a higher tip for exemplary service.

While tipping is not compulsory in Virginia, it is considered customary and expected as a reward for good service. However, if the service obtained is inadequate, it is appropriate to speak with a manager or supervisor to rectify any issues.

Conclusion

Finally, the "Update Virginia Travel Guide 2023" is an excellent resource for visitors interested in learning more about the state's history, culture, and natural beauty. Because of its extensive coverage of the state's past and present, as well as its concentration on outdoor activities, it is an excellent resource for both explorers and history buffs. However, some readers may find its lack of coverage of urban areas to be a detriment. Despite this issue, the booklet provides a full and informative introduction to Virginia and is highly recommended for anyone thinking about visiting the state.

Made in the USA
Monee, IL
02 July 2023